225 Pius IV (1559-1565)
226 St. Pius V
(1566-1572)
227 Gregory XIII
(1572-1585)
228 Sixtus V (1585-1590)
229 Urban VII (1590)
230 Gregory XIV
(1590-1591)
231 Innocent IX (1591)
232 Clement VIII
(1592-1605)
233 Leo XI (1605)
234 Paul V (1605-1621)
235 Gregory XV
(1621-1623)
236 Urban VIII
(1623-1644)
237 Innocent X
(1644-1655)
238 Alexander VII
(1655-1667)
239 Clement IX
(1667-1669)
240 Clement X
(1670-1676)
241 Blessed Innocent XI
(1676-1689)
242 Alexander VIII
(1689-1691)
243 Innocent XII
(1691-1700)
244 Clement XI
(1700-1721)
245 Innocent XIII
(1721-1724)
246 Benedict XIII
(1724-1730)
247 Clement XII
(1730-1740)
248 Benedict XIV
(1740-1758)
249 Clement XIII
(1758-1769)
250 Clement XIV
(1769-1774)
251 Pius VI (1775-1799)
252 Pius VII (1800-1823)
253 Leo XII (1823-1829)
254 Pius VIII (1829-1830)
255 Gregory XVI
(1831-1846)
256 Blessed Pius IX
(1846-1878)
257 Leo XIII (1878-1903)
258 St. Pius X
(1903-1914)
259 Benedict XV
(1914-1922)
260 Pius XI (1922-39)
261 Pius XII (1939-1958)
262 Blessed John XXIII
(1958-1963)
263 Paul VI (1963-1978)
264 John Paul I (1978)
265 John Paul II (1978—

ROMAN EMPERORS

1 Augustus (Octavian)
(27BC-AD14)
2 Tiberius (14-37)
3 Caligula (Gaius) (37-41)
4 Claudius (41-54)
5 Nero (54-68)
6 Galba (68-69)
7 Otho (69)
8 Vitellius (69)
9 Vespasian (69-79)

10 Titus (79-81)
11 Domitian (81-96)
12 Nerva (96-98)
13 Trajan (98-117)
14 Hadrian (117-138)
15 Antoninus Pius
(138-161)
16 Marcus Aurelius
(161-180)
17 Lucius Aurelius Verus
(161-169)
18 Commodus (180-192)
19 Pertinax (193)
20 Didius Julian (193)
21 Septimius Severus
(193-211)
22 Caracalla (211-217)
23 Macrinus (217-218)
24 Elagabalus (218-222)
25 Alexander Severus
(222-235)
26 Maximinus (235-238)
27 Gordian (238)
28 Gordian II (238)
29 Pupienus (238)
30 Balbinus (238)
31 Gordian III (238-244)
32 Philip 'the Arab'
(244-249)
33 Decius (249-251)
34 Gallus (251-253)
35 Aemilian (253)
36 Valerian (253-259)
37 Gallienus (259-268)
38 Claudius II (268-270)
39 Aurelian (270-275)
40 Tacitus (275-276)
41 Florian (276)
42 Probus (276-282)
43 Carus (282-283)
44 Numerian (283-284)
45 Carinus (283-285)
46 Diocletian (284-305)
47 Maximian (286-305)
48 Constantius I (305-306)
49 Galerius (305-311)
50 Constantine I, the Great
(311-337)
51 Constantine II
(337-340)
52 Constantius II
(337-361)
53 Constans (337-350)
54 Julian, the Apostate
(361-363)
55 Jovian (363-364)
56 Valentinian I
(in the West)
(364-375)
57 Valens (in the East)
(364-378)
58 Gratian (in the West)
(375-383)
59 Valentinian II
(in the West)
(375-392)
60 Theodosius, the Great
(in the East, and after
394, in the West)
(379-395)
61 Maximus (in the West)
(383-388)

65 Constantius III
(co-emperor in the
West)
(421)
66 Theodosius II
(in the East)
(408-450)
67 Valentinian III
(in the West)
(425-455)
68 Marcian (in the East)
(450-457)
69 Petronius (in the West)
(455)
70 Avitus (in the West)
(455-456)
71 Majorian (in the West)
(457-461)
72 Leo I (in the East)
(457-474)
73 Severus (in the West)
(461-465)
74 Anthemius
(in the West)
(467-472)
75 Olybrius (in the West)
(472)
76 Glycerius (in the West)
(473)
77 Julius Nepos
(in the West)
(473-475)
78 Leo II (in the East)
(473-474)
79 Zeno (in the East)
(474-491)
80 Romulus Augustulus
(in the West) (475-476)

HOLY ROMAN EMPERORS FRANKISH KINGS AND EMPERORS (CAROLINGIAN)

1 Charlemagne (800-814)
2 Louis I, the Pious
(814-840)
3 Lothair I (840-855)
4 Louis II (855-875)
5 Charles II, the Bald
(875-877)
6 Throne vacant (877-881)
7 Charles III, the Fat
(881-887)
8 Throne vacant (887-891)
9 Guido of Spoleto
(891-894)
10 Lambert of Spoleto
(co-emperor)
(892-898)
11 Arnulf (rival) (896-901)
12 Louis III of Provence
(901-905)
13 Berengar (905-924)
14 Conrad I of Franconia
(rival) (911-918)

SAXON KINGS AND EMPERORS

1 Henry I, the Fowler
(919-936)

FRANCONIAN EMPERORS (SALIAN)

1 Conrad II, the Salian
(1024-1039)
2 Henry III, the Black
(1039-1056)
3 Henry IV (1056-1106)
4 Rudolf of Swabia (rival)
(1077-1080)
5 Hermann of Luxembourg
(rival)
(1081-1093)
6 Conrad of Franconia
(rival)
(1093-1101)
7 Henry V (1106-1125)
8 Lothair II (1125-1137)

HOHENSTAUFEN KINGS AND EMPERORS

1 Conrad III (1138-1152)
2 Frederick Barbarossa
(1152-1190)
3 Henry VI (1190-1197)
4 Otto IV (1198-1215)
5 Philip of Swabia (rival)
(1198-1208)
6 Frederick II (1215-1250)
7 Henry Raspe (rival)
(1246-1247)
8 William of Holland (rival)
(1247-1256)
9 Conrad IV (1250-1254)
The Great Interregnum
(1254-1273)

RULERS FROM DIFFERENT HOUSES

1 Richard of Cornwall
(rival) (1257-1272)
2 Alfonso X of Castile
(rival) (1257-1273)
3 Rudolf I, Habsburg
(1273-1291)
4 Adolf I of Nassau
(1292-1298)
5 Albert I, Habsburg
(1298-1308)
6 Henry VII, Luxembourg
(1308-1313)
7 Louis IV of Bavaria
(1314-1347)
8 Frederick of Habsburg
(co-Regent) (1314-1325)
9 Charles IV, Luxembourg
(1347-1378)
10 Wenceslas of Bohemia
(1378-1400)
11 Frederick III of
Brunswick (1400)
12 Rupert of the Palatinate
(1400-1410)
13 Sigismund, Luxembourg
(1410-1437)

HABSBURG EMPERORS

1 Albert II (1438-1439)
2 Frederick III (1440-1493)
3 Maximilian I (1493-1519)
4 Charles V (1519-1558)
5 Ferdinand I (1558-1564)
6 Maximilian II
(1564-1576)
7 Rudolf II (1576-1612)
8 Matthias (1612-1619)

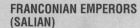

Brain Power

Time Lines

World History Dates

Penny Clarke

BOOK HOUSE

Contents

Due to the changing nature of internet links, Book House has developed an online list of websites related to the subject of this book. This site is updated regularly. Please use this link to access the list:
http://www.book-house.co.uk/bp/timelines

Glaciers/sea ice
Tundra
Rainforest
Woodland forest
Grass-scrub
Desert
Spread of humans

1,800,000 BC The first recognisable people are living in Africa. Archaeologists named them *Homo erectus* because they are the first people who we know walked upright (erect).

500,000 BC The discovery of fire was enormously important. Now people could eat food that had been too tough or even poisonous to eat raw. Fire also helped them to live in places that had been too cold for them before.

TIME AND DATES

Can you imagine living without time? Living without knowing what day it is, or what month or year? The first people knew the time of day from the sun's position and understood the passing of the seasons, but that was all. They could not read or write, so could not leave records of when they made a cave painting or a tool. So the dates on these two pages cannot be exact.

Famous figures

50,000 BC Fossils show that modern human beings like us (*Homo sapiens sapiens*) had developed.

35,000 BC To live in cold places people need shelters as well as fire. In Russia there are remains of round houses from this time.

30,000 BC As people move northward to places with long dark winter days, they need light. Fires give some, but lamps burning fat or oil give a steadier light.

32,000 BC Stone is carefully flaked into sharp tools to skin and cut up the hunters' catch. The meat is eaten and the skins used for clothes and handles for tools.

20,000 BC Deep in caves artists are painting magnificent pictures of the animals they see and hunt. Why? The pictures are so well hidden, experts think they were painted for religious purposes.

20,000 BC Holding the tips of wooden spears in fire hardens them. This makes them sharper and so better weapons, both for hunting animals and attacking other people.

There is no written evidence from this distant time so we know nothing about individual people. We rely on what archaeologists and other specialists find for our knowledge of the time. But a great deal has been destroyed – and not everything has been found!

There's also another problem – how do we know what we're looking at? This figure of a pregnant woman was made about 25,000 BC, but was she a real person or a mythical goddess? Pregnancy and birth were often linked with goddesses of spring.

In the same way no-one knows who created the animal paintings in the French caves or the Sahara Desert, or why. There are many theories, but that is not the same as knowing for sure!

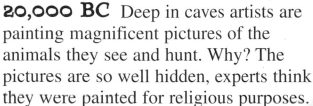

THE FIRST CIVILISATIONS

The Great Pyramid at Giza in Egypt was built by the Pharaoh Cheops over 4000 years ago. It is the largest stone structure in the world. The Ancient Egyptians believed that their pharaoh was Horus, the son of Re, the sun god. When the pharaoh died he would cross over into the land of the dead, where he would be reunited with his father. Since their god-king lived forever, the Egyptians believed he would bless and protect them with good harvests and victories in battle as long as they preserved his body. The pyramids, with their deep, hidden burial chambers, were designed to do this and protect the pharaoh's body forever.

A date to remember

2600-2560 BC

The pyramids were built

Time Line

c.6000 BC Farming communities grow up in Anatolia (modern Turkey).

c.4000 BC In India farming communities are growing up in the valley of the River Indus.

c.4000 BC The first huge stone monuments that archaeologists call megaliths are built in Malta, Brittany (France) and the Iberian Peninsula (modern Spain and Portugal).

c.3400 The potter's wheel is invented in the rich city-state of Sumer (in part of modern Iraq). This invention makes it quicker and easier to work clay.

3118 BC Menes becomes the first pharaoh of Egypt when he unites the two kingdoms of Upper Egypt and Lower Egypt.

c.3000 BC Farming communities grow up in Mexico and Peru.

c.3000 BC Olives and vines are being grown in what is now Greece.

You'r running late!

Yes, we have a deadline!

6

Important events

6000 BC Catal Hüyük is built in southern Turkey. The houses are very close together for strength and safety. Visitors enter and exit through a trapdoor in the roof.

4000-3000 BC Cave paintings in the Sahara Desert show people herding cattle.

3500 BC Ancient Sumerian works of art show wheeled carts drawn by oxen or donkeys. This proves they are being used at this time.

Ancient clay writing tablet

3500 BC Writing is invented in Sumeria. People use a reed stylus to make marks in soft clay tablets.

Ancient Sumerian relief showing domestic animals

3000 BC Sumerian people have domesticated cows and sheep, which provide them with milk, cheese, meat and hides.

3000 BC The Ancient Egyptians develop the art of building with cut stone. They build the great pyramids to provide grand burial sites for their pharaohs.

Famous figures

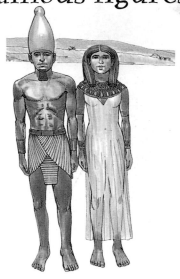

As rulers of Egypt, the pharaohs had many responsibilities: deciding on government policy, overseeing officials, keeping law and order, making allies, and sometimes leading armies into battle against enemies. An Egyptian pharaoh was more than a king – he acted as a representative for the gods on earth, and would consult them every day in their temples. Most pharaohs were men, although there were a few women rulers, such as Queen Hatshepsut (c.1503-1482 BC) (page 11). In her reign Hatshepsut promoted exploration and long-distance trade with states in Africa, south of Egypt. The beautiful Cleopatra VII was the last queen to rule Egypt (48-30 BC). She tried in vain to stop the Romans invading Egypt, but when they did, she killed herself instead of surrendering to Roman rule.

3000 to 1700 BC
CHARIOTS AND WARS

The land between the two great rivers, the Tigris and Euphrates, is extremely fertile. (It is now modern Iraq.) The Sumerians were just one of the wealthy and successful peoples who settled in the region and built up a strong city-state. As well as inventing writing and the wheel (pages 6 and 7), the Sumerians built great palaces and temples of mud bricks. Mud bricks are not as strong as stone, so few of the Sumerians' buildings survive – in contrast to those of the Ancient Egyptians.

As kingdoms and city-states grew in size and wealth, they began to see neighbouring states as rivals. This led to wars between states. At first these were fought on foot, but then someone, somewhere, realised that slow, clumsy ox-carts could be adapted to make battle transport – at least for the leaders. And so fast, light chariots came into use.

A date to remember
C.2500 BC
Sumerian civilisation

In the East, various kingdoms fought over the region's fertile lands, trade routes and gold and silver deposits. Eventually, in c.2500 BC, King Ur united the warring states and they became known as the Sumerians.

Time Line

C.3000 BC People living on the islands of Japan are using pottery.

C.3000 BC The Cochise hunter-gatherer people are living in south-western North America.

C.2500 BC People in northern Europe begin to use bronze.

C.2000 BC Horses are being trained to pull chariots.

C.2000 BC Stonehenge is built in what is now southern England.

C.2000 BC The Hittites, a people from the east, invade Anatolia (part of modern Turkey). From c.1450–1200 BC their empire stretches from the Mediterranean Sea to the Persian Gulf.

C.1700 BC On Crete the Mycenean people are using the writing called Linear A in their great civilisation.

Important events

The shaduf

2600 BC The wealth of Sumerian cities makes them important trade centres.

2500 BC The shaduf – a long pole with a weight at one end and a bucket at the other – is invented. It makes watering crops much easier.

C.2500 BC The great Indus Valley civilisation begins to become powerful. Harappa and Mohenjo-Daro are its most important cities.

2000 BC Looms are being used in Egypt. Only the pharaoh, his family, and top officials can wear clothes of the finest linen.

2000 BC In China the Shang dynasty takes power. Their chariots have spoked wheels.

Famous figures

Prince Gilgamesh (ruled some time between 3000 and 2000 BC)
The rulers of wealthy city-states needed to keep records, especially of tax payments. Once writing developed this was easy, and they employed scribes, people who could read and write, to keep the records. The scribes always included the ruler's name, so we begin to learn about actual people. One, Prince Gilgamesh, ruled Uruk (in modern Iraq).

C.2500 BC
The centre of Gilgamesh's power was the city of Uruk. Behind its high mud-brick walls were splendid temples and palaces. Many of the temples or ziggurats were built as a series of terraces. Only the high priest and the ruler could enter the topmost part of the temple, which was the holiest because it was nearest the heavens.

9

1700 BC to 800 BC
LONG LIVE THE PHARAOH

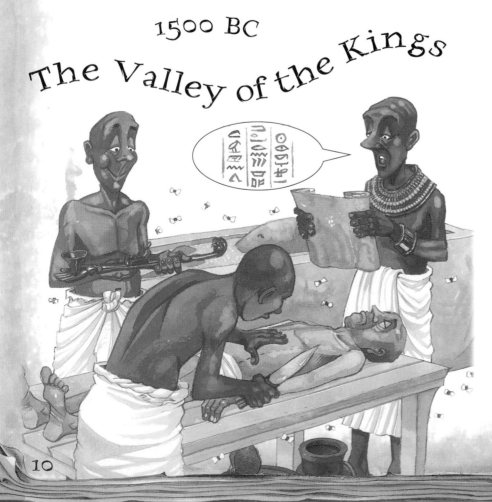

Around 1500 BC, the time begins in Egyptian history that scholars call the New Kingdom. In this period three generations of Egyptian pharaohs rose to power. One of these, Tuthmosis I, was the first to have his tomb cut into the rocks of the Valley of the Kings – the royal burial place on the west bank of the Nile, opposite the capital city of Thebes. The Egyptians preserved bodies by a process of embalming and mummification. The dead were taken across the river to an embalmer who dried, preserved and wrapped the body in strips of linen, a process taking about 70 days. Then the mummified body was put in its coffin and carried to its tomb in a procession of mourners and priests.

A date to remember

1500 BC

The Valley of the Kings

Time Line

c.1700 BC In Peru people are settling in large permanent villages.

c.1500 BC In India floods destroy the Indus Valley civilisation. The Hindu religion develops.

c.1500 BC The Olmecs living in part of what is now modern Mexico are using hieroglyphic writing.

c.1500 BC Cattle are domesticated in Africa.

c.1400 BC On Crete, Linear B (an early form of Greek) is being used.

c.1370-1353 BC Pharaoh Akhenaten of Egypt introduces a new religion with only one god.

c.1250 BC City of Troy destroyed by the Greeks, so ending the Trojan Wars.

c.1028 BC In China the Shang rulers are replaced by the Chou dynasty.

c.1000 BC In Central America the Mayas build large temples on terraces.

Important events

Hatshepsut's temple

Queen Hatshepsut

1480 BC Queen Hatshepsut builds a temple in honour of her reign.

1425-1417 BC Years of war between Egypt and Mesopotamia end when Pharaoh Tuthmosis IV marries a princess from Mitanni (in modern Syria).

1500 BC Bull-leaping is an important part of the religious ceremonies performed in the royal palaces, such as Knossos, in Crete.

Bull-leaping ceremony

1000 BC Arabian countries like Phoenicia (modern Lebanon) and Persia (Iran) are strong and wealthy because they have valuable natural resources which they trade with Egypt and other lands in the Middle East.

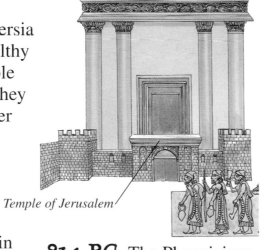

Temple of Jerusalem

974-937 BC King Solomon is ruler of the Jews. He builds a magnificent new temple in the holy city of Jerusalem.

Stone carving of Phoenician trading ships

814 BC The Phoenicians found the city of Carthage in Tunisia, North Africa. Hannibal, the military hero who crossed the Alps with elephants to fight the Romans, is born here.

Famous figures

Queen Hatshepsut (ruled c.1503-1482 BC)
She was one of the very few women to rule Egypt.

Pharaoh Akhenaten (ruled c.1370-1353 BC)
Founder of a new religion and builder of a great new city.

Queen Nefertiti
She was the beautiful wife of Pharaoh Akhenaten.

Pharaoh Tutankhamen (ruled 1336-1327 BC)
The splendid tomb of this young pharaoh remained undiscovered until AD 1922.

Pharaoh Ramses II (ruled 1290-1224 BC)
One of the greatest pharaohs, he built many huge temples.

THE BIRTH OF DEMOCRACY

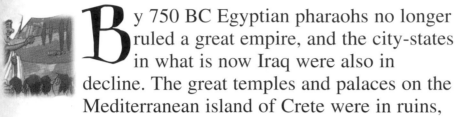

By 750 BC Egyptian pharaohs no longer ruled a great empire, and the city-states in what is now Iraq were also in decline. The great temples and palaces on the Mediterranean island of Crete were in ruins, and the Linear B alphabet had been forgotten.

The Phoenicians (based in modern Lebanon) were great seafarers. Slowly they rebuilt trade with mainland Greece, where small new city-states, such as Athens, Corinth and Sparta, grew up around the old strongholds. Many of these city-states were ruled by groups of citizens, not kings. Athens became a democracy (from a Greek word meaning 'rule by the people'). A governing assembly was held every nine days and every citizen could vote at it. However, only men born in Athens could be citizens, so in modern terms Athens was not a real democracy.

Time Line

c.725 BC A new, simpler alphabet, based on the one used by the Phoenicians, is adopted.

586 BC Nebuchadnezzar II, king of Babylon, destroys Jerusalem. He starts building the Hanging Gardens of Babylon, one of the Wonders of the World.

563 BC Prince Siddhartha Gautama is born. He later becomes the Buddha (Enlightened One).

470 BC Hanno of Carthage sails down the west coast of Africa.

c.450 BC The Nok civilisation in Nigeria grows more powerful.

A date to remember
594 BC
The Hanging Gardens of Babylon

Important events

753 BC Romulus and Remus found Rome.

500 BC The Etruscans (above), who settled in northern Italy c.900 BC, are at their most powerful. Soon the Romans will replace them.

683 BC Athens replaces its hereditary kings with *archons* (chief magistrates).

c.600 BC Lycurgus (left) lays down the laws of Sparta.

c.480 BC The *bouleterion*, the council chamber of the Athenian assembly (above). Meetings are held every nine days, but citizens do not have to attend.

447 BC Pericles orders the building of a magnificent temple to Athene, Athens' goddess and protector. The temple, the Parthenon, is built on the Acropolis, the highest point in the city. Over two thousand years later it still stands, dominating the modern city of Athens.

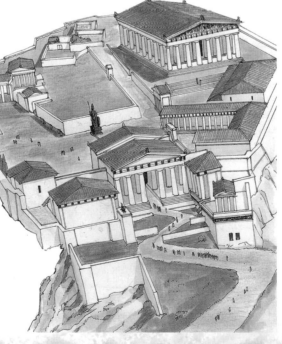

Famous figures

Pericles (leader 495-429 BC) Pericles successfully led the Athenians in war. At home, he encouraged art and culture.

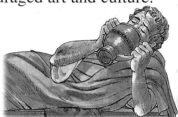

Socrates (469-399 BC) One of Athens' most important philosophers, he attacked political corruption. This made enemies for him. He was tried on false charges and forced to drink poison.

Hippocrates (c.460-377 BC) A Greek doctor regarded as the father of modern medicine. He is believed to have been the first person to study patients and their symptoms closely and to describe how he treated them.

350 to 100 BC
EMPIRES RISE AND FALL

Look back at almost any period in the past and you will find upheavals and wars in some part of the world. The years between 350 and 100 BC are no exception. Right across the world empires declined and others rose to replace them. From around 300 BC the Maya replaced the once-powerful Olmecs in part of modern Mexico and built up an even larger empire. In Europe the Romans attacked the Carthaginians in North Africa who, in turn, attacked the Romans. In China, Emperor Wu-ti's road and canal-building programme was helping him extend the boundaries of his empire, just as it had helped the Romans extend theirs. The Persians occupied Egypt more than once. But the greatest empire was Alexander the Great's. When he died in 323 BC it stretched eastwards from Greece all the way to the western border of India.

Time Line

336 BC Alexander the Great comes to power.

327-325 BC Alexander is fighting in India.

C.300 BC The Maya begin to build up their power in Middle America.

272 BC In India, King Asoka comes to the throne and starts to build his empire. He also becomes a Buddhist.

C.220 BC Emperor Zheng of China orders the building of a Great Wall to keep out northern tribes.

218 BC Hannibal of Carthage crosses the Alps and invades Italy.

C.170 BC Small Greek states are set up in the Punjab region of India.

150 BC After years of conflict, the Romans destroy the North African kingdom of Carthage.

140 BC The Chinese emperor Wu-ti conquers Korea and North Vietnam.

A date to remember 220 BC
The Great Wall of China

Heave!

14

Important events

C.340 BC Demosthenes tries to persuade his fellow Athenians to resist Phillip of Macedon's attacks. They ignore him.

336-323 BC Alexander, Phillip's son, builds up a huge empire, but it collapses when he dies in 323 BC.

C.292-280 BC A huge bronze statue of Helios, the sun god (left), is built on the Mediterranean island of Rhodes. It has one foot on each side of the harbour entrance and is nicknamed 'the Colossus of Rhodes'.

146 BC The last battle of the three Punic Wars between the Romans and Carthaginians takes place. Under their general, Scipio, the Romans win, destroying Carthage's power and taking over its colonies.

509-27 BC Rome is a republic (its last king was deposed in 509). However, most of the top government posts are still held by men from the richest, most important families.

Famous figures

Alexander the Great (ruled 336-323 BC)
An inspiring general and brilliant tactician, Alexander the Great broke the power of the Persians at the battle of Issus in 333 BC. After his victory he marched across their empire to India. This helped to spread Greek culture very widely.

Qin Shi Huang Di, emperor of China (dies 210 BC)
In life the first emperor of a united China commanded a huge army. In death he does so too, but this time they are life-size terracotta models buried with him in his tomb.

100 BC to AD 100
THE POWER OF ROME

During this time the Romans' grip on the known world was occasionally challenged, but never loosened. Their empire was at its largest in the reign of Trajan (AD 98-117), stretching from northern Britain eastwards across Europe and North Africa to the Black Sea. At home, however, matters were not always so peaceful. There were conflicts within the ruling elite, political assassinations, and even popular unrest.

The destruction of the wealthy cities of Pompeii and Herculaneum by the eruption of Vesuvius in 79 BC killed thousands of people and caused much unease. At the time no-one understood that such eruptions were natural events, instead they feared the gods were angry with them and their rulers.

A date to remember 79 BC
Vesuvius erupts!

Time Line

86 BC Han emperor Wu-ti of China dies, and a time of unrest begins.

55 BC Julius Caesar's invasion of Britain is unsuccessful.

30 BC Cleopatra, Queen of Egypt, commits suicide as her country becomes a Roman province.

27 BC Roman Republic ends. Octavian becomes the first Emperor of Rome.

c.5 BC Birth of Jesus in Bethlehem.

AD 25 Han dynasty regains power in China.

AD 43 The Romans conquer Britain.

AD 44 Romans conquer Mauretania (Morocco).

AD 61 Boudicca, queen of the Iceni, leads a revolt against Roman rule in Britain. The Iceni destroy Colchester and London before they are defeated.

16

Important events

73-71 BC Spartacus leads a revolt of 40,000 slaves. As punishment, 6,000 are crucified beside the main road into Rome.

44 BC Assassination of Julius Caesar by his enemies.

31 BC Battle of Actium: Romans defeat Egyptian rulers Cleopatra and Mark Antony.

c.5 BC Wise men from the east visit Jesus.

AD 9 German tribes under Arminius wipe out three Roman legions – a blow to Rome.

AD 61 Another shock to Roman power is the revolt of the Iceni in eastern England, led by Queen Boudicca.

AD 73 Having destroyed the temple in Jerusalem in AD 70, the Romans take the Jewish stronghold of Masada. The defenders kill themselves.

AD 75 The Romans regard the new religion of Christianity as a threat and begin to persecute Christians. Pitting them against wild animals and armed gladiators becomes a popular spectator-sport in Rome's Colosseum.

Famous figures

Octavian/Augustus (ruled 27 BC-AD 14) The unrest following Caesar's murder ended when Octavian took power as Emperor Augustus.

Tiberius (ruled AD 14-37) He succeeded Augustus, his father-in-law, as Emperor of Rome.

Nero (ruled AD 54-68) Nero, stepson and heir of Emperor Claudius, comes to power after his stepfather is murdered by his wife (Nero's mother). Increasingly cruel and unstable, he faces revolts abroad and intrigues at home. He finally commits suicide.

100 to 350
POWERS IN DECLINE

Although the Roman Empire was at its largest from AD 98 to 117, it was increasingly under pressure. Attacks by peoples on its boundaries, especially in northern Britain, northern Germany and near the Black Sea, were an increasing nuisance and drain on military resources. And not all Roman emperors were good rulers, some were weak, others corrupt, and some were both weak and corrupt.

Similar things were occurring elsewhere in the world too. In Africa the kingdom of Nubia was conquered by the ruler of Axum (Ethiopia), so becoming the major power in the region by the Red Sea. In northern China, tribes from Central Asia broke through the Great Wall, ending China's feeling of security.

A date to remember 100

Introduction of Buddhism into China

Time Line

c. AD 100 Paper is invented in China.

c.180 In Japan different tribes begin uniting into larger groups.

c.195 India is invaded by tribes from Parthia near the Caspian Sea. They hold power for over 200 years.

200 After 700 years the Nok civilisation in Nigeria comes to an end.

c.250 In Central America Mayan astronomers make complex mathematical calculations.

260 Shapur I of Persia defeats the Romans and captures Emperor Valerian.

268-73 Queen Zenobia of Palmyra conquers parts of the Roman Empire in the Middle East.

316 Empress Jingo of Japan invades Korea.

320 Chandragupta II founds the Gupta Empire in India. It will be a time of great cultural flowering.

Important events

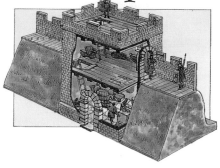

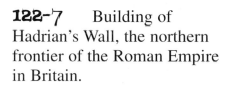
122-7 Building of Hadrian's Wall, the northern frontier of the Roman Empire in Britain.

161-80 Reign of Emperor Marcus Aurelius. Increasing attacks by German tribes threaten the empire's northern frontier.

211-17 Reign of the cruel and corrupt Emperor Caracalla (left).

235 As the empire comes under increasing threat, so the political tensions in Rome also increase.

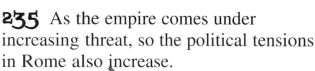

270 Emperor Aurelian, who rose from being an ordinary soldier, abandons Dacia (north-west Romania) to the Goths tribes.

286 In the face of the growing number of attacks on the empire, Diocletian divides it in two. He appoints Maximian as his co-emperor to rule the western half, while he rules the eastern half.

Famous figures

Trajan (ruled 98-117)
A good general and popular emperor, Trajan made many social reforms. He also conquered Dacia (north-west Romania), making it a Roman province.

Hadrian (ruled 117-38)
Trajan's adopted son and heir, Hadrian saw it as his duty to make the empire's boundaries secure. Hadrian's Wall was built for this reason in what is now the north of England.

Diocletian (ruled 284-305)
By dividing the empire he was admitting its weakness. Christians suffered much persecution during his rule.

Constantine (ruled 306-337)
In 330 he moved the Empire's capital from Rome to Byzantium, renaming the city Constantinopolos. Later it became Constantinople and is now Istanbul.

THE END OF AN EMPIRE

The Roman Empire, the dominant power in Europe, North Africa and much of the Middle East for so long, collapsed in the fifth century AD. Attacks by Goths and Vandals, tribes from northern Europe, first forced the Romans to abandon their Empire's outlying provinces. Then, in 410, the Goths sacked Rome, the capital city and centre of power. This devastating blow was repeated in 455 when the Vandals destroyed the city. Finally, in 476, the western part of the Roman Empire ceased to exist, although, the eastern part, the Byzantine Empire, lasted another thousand years. As the Romans' power collapsed, new, smaller kingdoms rose in their old lands, including eastern and western France, Britain, North Africa and Italy itself.

A date to remember 410
The Goths sack Rome

thwack

crumbs!

Time Line

C.370 The Huns, nomadic people from central Asia, attack Europe.

391 Christianity becomes the state religion of the Roman Empire under the Emperor Theodosius.

C.400 The Incas begin to establish their power in South America.

430-470 Attacks by the Huns cause the Gupta Empire's decline in India.

531 Byzantine emperor Justinian sends Christian missionaries to Axum (in modern-day Ethiopia).

C.537 Alfred, king of the Britons, killed in the Battle of Camlan.

C.600 Mayan civilisation at its most powerful in Central America.

624 Buddhism becomes China's official religion.

632 Mohammed, founder of Islam, dies.

640 Arabs occupy Egypt.

Important events

434-53 Reign of Attila (right), king of the Huns, who laid waste large parts of Europe.

493 Theodoric, king of the Ostrogoths (eastern Goths), sets up a kingdom in Italy.

534-7 Hagia Sophia is built in Constantinople. It has the world's biggest dome.

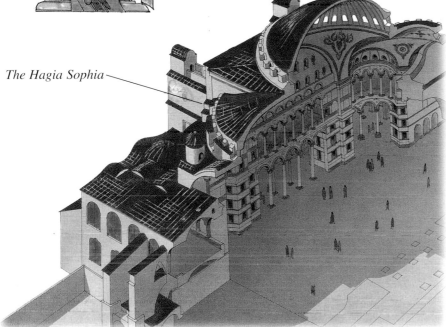

The Hagia Sophia

C.627 Death of Raewald, possible ruler of East Anglia. The magnificent treasures, including this helmet (below), in the ship burial at Sutton Hoo, Suffolk, show that it may be his grave.

629-39 Reign of Dagobert, king of the Franks. He reunites all the Frankish peoples, making them a powerful force in Europe.

640 The Christian Byzantine Empire comes under increasing attack from the Muslim Arabs.

Famous figures

Mohammed (570-632)
Born in the Arabian city of Mecca, Mohammed founded Islam, one of the world's great religions. His teaching that there was only one God was unpopular.

The Hegira – 622
Mohammed's teachings were so unpopular, that in 622 he and his followers fled from Mecca. They went to Medina, another Arabian city.

The return to Mecca – 630
After many struggles, Mohammed returned to Mecca, establishing it as the centre of Islam, with the stone Kaaba (below) as its heart.

640 to 899
LAND AND SEA RAIDERS

Throughout the eighth and ninth centuries the peoples of Europe lived in fear of attack. In the north and west the attackers were seafaring Vikings from Scandinavia, while in the south and west it was powerful Muslim rulers. By 711 most of Spain was in Muslim hands and only losing the Battle of Poitiers in 732 stopped the Muslims advancing further into France.

Life in the Vikings' northern homelands was harsh, so raiding rich, undefended targets like Christian monasteries was an easier way to make a living. The first raid, in 793, was on the monasteries of Lindisfarne and Jarrow in north-east England. Every summer after that (the sea was too rough in winter) people living by the coast anxiously scanned the horizon hoping they would not see the sails of the pagan Vikings' longships.

711-1236 The Moors rule Cordoba in Spain. The Great Mosque is the finest of the many magnificent buildings they constructed.

A date to remember 711

The Moors invade Spain

Time Line

649 Emperor T'ai Tsung the Great of China dies.

661 The Omayyad dynasty of Islamic rulers comes to power in Damascus (Syria).

663 The Japanese finally end occupation of Korea.

674-8 The Arabs besiege Constantinople.

c.700 Anasazi farmers appear in North America.

702 Arabic becomes the official language of Egypt.

711 Arabs conquer Spain.

756 Papal States founded in Italy.

793 Vikings raid the Northumbrian coast.

814 Baghdad, capital of the Islamic caliphs, is the world's largest city.

850 The great Acropolis of Zimbabwe is built.

861 The Vikings reach Iceland.

Important events

627-49 Emperor T'ai Tsung rules China. To claim the throne he murdered his brothers and made his father abdicate.

661 Ali, son-in-law of Mohammed and leader of the Islamic world, is murdered. As a result his followers, the Shi'ites, break away from the rest of the Islamic world.

732 Charles Martel wins the Battle of Poitiers, stopping Muslim forces advancing further into Europe.

755 Ming Huang, Emperor of China for 44 years, is forced to abdicate and flee. The new emperor is An Lushan, a rebel general who is himself murdered in 757.

779 Offa, King of Mercia, becomes ruler of England. In 757 he had built a dyke (ditch) to stop Welsh invasions.

787 Members of the early Christian Church meet at Nicaea in the reign of Constantine VI.

871-99 Alfred the Great rules Wessex and stops the Danes advancing further west into Britain.

882 The Viking Oleg the Wise takes Kiev and makes it the capital of Russia.

895 Paris is besieged by the Vikings, who settle at the mouth of the River Seine in 896.

Famous figures

Charlemagne (ruled 771-814)
Conquered much of Europe and founded the Holy Roman Empire.

Bringer of law and justice
Charlemagne sent judges all over his kingdom to administer justice and his laws.

A Christian ruler
Charlemagne forced his subjects to become Christian, although many were pagans.

The law-maker
To stamp his authority on his empire, Charlemagne made new laws and sent out his officials to enforce them.

RAIDERS TO RULERS

By the end of the ninth century, Muslim rulers were in power from the Spanish peninsula in the west to Afghanistan in the east. (In 751 they had even won a victory over the Chinese.) They allowed Christians and Jews to practise their religions freely, and encouraged scholarship and medicine.

Further north in Europe the picture was different. During the ninth and tenth centuries Viking attacks on Britain and north-western Europe were at their peak. But, very gradually, the Vikings changed from raiders to traders and, finally, they settled in the lands their ancestors had once attacked. Because they came from the north, the Vikings were also called Northmen or Norsemen. By the eleventh century those living in northern France were called Normans.

A date to remember 1000
Vikings land in America

...and **don't** come back!

Time Line

C.900 Harald Finehair unites Norway into one kingdom.

900 The Maya emigrate to the Yucatan, Central America.

907 Civil war in China.

920 Empire of Ghana at its height.

982 The Viking Erik the Red founds a colony in Greenland.

990 Yangtu (the future Beijing) becomes the capital of northern China.

C.1000 The Chinese invent gunpowder.

C.1000 Leif Eriksson, Erik the Red's son, reaches North America.

1016 Canute (Cnut) of Denmark becomes king of England.

1016 Sicily is invaded by the Normans.

Important events

899 King Alfred of Wessex dies. He had ended the Vikings' advance.

C.900 The tomb (left) of Isma'il, ruler of a Central Asian kingdom.

922 Ibn Fadlan, the ambassador of the caliph (Islamic ruler) of Baghdad, sees and describes a Viking funeral on the banks of the River Volga in Russia.

C.967 Fatimid dynasty is established in Egypt and Islamic power stretches across North Africa.

1003 Swein Forkbeard, King of Denmark, attacks England in revenge for the murder of his sister.

1013 Swein captures London.

1042 Edward the Confessor comes to the English throne.

Famous figures

Henry I (ruled 919-36)
Henry, nicknamed 'the Fowler', rules the Saxon lands in Germany. When he dies in 936 his son, Otto, succeeds him, so establishing a hereditary kingdom.

Harald Bluetooth (ruled c.950-86)
Around 960 Harald, King of Denmark, becomes a Christian, the first Viking ruler to do so. It is rumoured that it is part of a peace treaty after Harald's defeat by Otto, the king of Germany.

Vladimir the Great (ruled 980-1015)
In 989 Vladimir, Grand Prince of Kiev, becomes a Christian after marrying a Byzantine princess. He forces all his people to convert too, leading them in a mass baptism in the River Dnieper.

WARS OF RELIGION

The Turks' growing power caused problems for Christians in the lands they conquered. The Turks were far less tolerant than the early Muslim rulers and began persecuting Christians. In 1095 the Byzantine emperor appealed for help to Pope Urban II, the head of the Christian church. The Pope preached a crusade or holy war against the Turks. Thousands answered his call, some for religious reasons, but many because it was a chance to gain land and wealth.

Thousands of miles away, in the Asian kingdom of Cambodia, a huge temple is being built at Angkor Wat, capital of the Khmer empire. It is a monument to King Suryavarman II, who made the empire larger than it had ever been before.

A date to remember
1150
Angkor Wat is finished

Time Line

1066 The Battle of Hastings. William of Normandy defeats Harold of England and becomes William I of England.

1071 Seljuk Turks capture Jerusalem.

1086 William orders the recording of property ownership in England – *The Domesday Book*.

1094 Portugal becomes an independent kingdom.

1095 The First Crusade.

C.1100 Kingdom of Ife in Nigeria grows in size and wealth.

1147 Second Crusade begins.

C.1150 Founding of Paris University.

1151 Toltec Empire ends in Mexico.

1156 Civil war in Japan.

1169 Saladin takes power in Egypt. He will be the Christians' dreaded enemy.

Important events

1066 Edward the Confessor, last Anglo-Saxon king of England, dies.

1071 Turks threatened by the Byzantine emperor get help from Sultan Alp Arslan (left).

1095 At Clermont, France, Pope Urban II (right) appeals to Christians to go to the Holy Land to rescue the Holy Places (those associated with Jesus Christ) from the Turks.

1099 The Crusaders capture Jerusalem from the Turks.

1135 Stephen, grandson of William the Conqueror, seizes the English throne from Queen Matilda. Civil war rages until her defeat in 1148.

1170 Thomas à Becket, Archbishop of Canterbury, is murdered on the orders of Henry II (left). The Pope makes him a saint in 1173.

1177 Pope Alexander III wins his power struggle with Emperor Frederick I of Germany (right). The Emperor has to agree that it is the cardinals who choose popes, not emperors.

Famous figures

Roger II of Sicily (ruled 1130-54) Norman king who encouraged art and learning.

Melisande (ruled 1143-52) Queen of Jerusalem, she rules with her son, Baldwin III, until he exiles her.

Saladin (ruled 1174-93) A great military leader, he was respected for his fairness.

Frederick I 'Barbarossa' (ruled 1152-90) His red beard earned him his nickname.

1180 to 1300
WARFARE AND RIGHTS

Many Crusaders (the soldiers who took part in the Crusades against the Muslims) never went home. They stayed in the Holy Land because the climate was better and the region much richer than the lands they came from. And there were no kings, so ambitious noblemen could grab land and power in a way they could not at home. Many nobles who did return were restless. They had probably been away for years and led armies successfully without their king interfering. If, when they returned, they found a weak ruler they often tried to reduce his power and increase theirs.

A date to remember 1215
Magna Carta

King John ruled England from 1199 to 1216. He was nicknamed 'Lackland' for losing most of England's lands in France. The barons (nobles) hated him because he taxed them to pay for his French wars. After a long struggle they forced him to sign Magna Carta in 1215 (see below). John broke its terms, so starting a civil war.

Pesky barons!

Time Line

1189 Third Crusade begins.

1189 Last-known visit by Vikings to North America.

1190 The Mongol Empire grows in eastern Asia.

C.1200 Pueblo building in south-west North America at its peak.

1200 Jews given privileges in Morocco.

1202 Arabic (modern) numbers are introduced in Europe.

1204 Soldiers of the Fourth Crusade sack Constantinople.

1210 Mongols invade China.

1215 English nobles force King John to sign Magna Carta, a charter of political rights.

1234 Mongols overthrow Chin dynasty in China.

1295 Model Parliament of Edward I of England.

Important events

1185 In Japan Moshitsuma Minamoto overthrows the ruling Taira clan, founding a dynasty that rules until 1219.

1189-92 The Third Crusade, led by Richard I of England (right), Frederick I of Germany and Phillip II of France, fails to take Jerusalem from the Muslims led by Saladin (below).

1212 The Children's Crusade to the Holy Land. Most are sold as slaves before getting there.

1215 The Mongols sack Beijing (Peking), the Chinese capital.

1226-70 In his long reign, Louis IX of France (right) led two Crusades, the Sixth (1248-54) and the Seventh (1270) during which he died.

1236 Ferdinand III of Castile and Léon drives the Moors (Muslims) out of their capital city of Cordoba in Spain.

1261 The Byzantine emperor Michael VIII regains control of Constantinople.

1277 King Edward I of England takes Wales and builds many strong castles.

Famous figures

Marco Polo (1254-1324) The merchant Marco Polo travels from his home in Venice, Italy, to China.

Eleanor of Aquitaine (c.1122-1204) Wife of King Henry II of England.

Blanche of Castile (d. 1234) She became Queen of France when she married King Louis VIII of France in 1226.

St Elizabeth of Hungary (1207-31) After her husband died on his way to the Sixth Crusade she devoted her life to the poor.

1300 to 1401
PALACES AND PLAGUE

Throughout these years the Aztecs were expanding their empire in what we now call Mexico. Beginning with a few small states, they ruthlessly suppressed any tribes who opposed them until, by 1325, they dominated the region. The Aztecs forced the people they conquered to pay them tribute: gold, precious stones and other valuable goods. If they did not pay, there was always the threat of an Aztec invasion, and the fear of that was enough to make them pay what their conquerors demanded. Much of the tribute paid for the building of Tenochtitlán, the Aztecs' capital city with its huge palaces and temples.

As the Aztecs were building their magnificent city, western Asia and Europe were about to suffer something far more deadly than military attack: the plague (the Black Death).

A date to remember
C.1325 Aztecs rule Mexico

The Aztecs' growing power is reflected in the fine city of Tenochtitlán, which they began building around 1325. Guided by their chief, Tenoch, they build it on islands in the middle of Lake Texcoco. In years to come it will be built over by the Spanish and become Mexico City.

Time Line

1306 France expels Jews.

1312 Suppression of the Knights Templar, an order of religious knights.

C.1325 The Aztecs dominate Mexico.

1328 Duke Ivan I of Moscow expands his state's frontiers.

1333 In China about five million people die from famine and floods.

1347 The Black Death reaches Italy from the east.

1363 Tamurlane begins his conquest of Asia.

1387 Geoffrey Chaucer writes *The Canterbury Tales*.

1389 Turks win the Battle of Kosovo, gaining control of the Balkans.

1397 Portuguese explorers reach the Canary Islands.

1401 Tamurlane conquers Damascus and Baghdad.

Important events

C.1305 The empire of Benin is a growing power in southern Nigeria.

1313 After expelling the Jews and suppressing the Knights Templar, Philip the Fair of France orders all lepers to be burnt.

begging bowl

clapper

1314 King Robert the Bruce of Scotland leads his people's fight for independence from the English. He defeats the English at the Battle of Bannockburn.

1348 The Black Death reaches England. By 1351 it will kill one-third of the population of Europe.

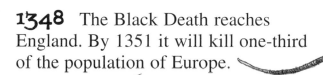

1356 Edward the Black Prince, heir of Edward III of England, defeats the French at Poitiers.

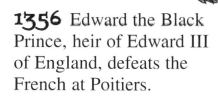

1381 Wat Tyler leads the Peasants' Revolt in England. He is murdered at a meeting with King Richard II.

1389 Bayezid I, founder of the Ottoman Empire, comes to power in Turkey.

1401 Owen Glendower leads a rebellion of the Welsh against the rule of the English king, Henry IV.

Famous figures

Edward III of England (ruled 1327-77)
In 1337, in an effort to regain English lands in France, Edward began the Hundred Years' War. In 1346 he defeated the French at Crécy.

Charles V 'the Wise' of France (ruled 1364-80)
A brilliant military commander, he regained most of the territory France had lost to England during the campaigns of King Edward III.

Grand Prince Dimitri of Moscow (ruled 1359-89)
Moscow had been part of the Mongols' huge empire since 1240. But their power was waning and Prince Dimitri and his army won a major victory over them in 1380.

AN AGE OF EXPLORATION

For thousands of years people had thought that the world was flat. But, by the end of the fifteenth century, most educated people realised it was really a sphere. So anyone sailing east (or west) would eventually arrive back where they had started. This was enormously important for European trade. Some of the most valuable trade goods were the spices used in cooking. They were very expensive, largely because they had to be brought great distances overland from the east, changing hands many times and becoming more expensive each time they did so. However, anyone sailing west would reach the Indies, the source of the spices, in the east. They could buy spices and bring them back to Europe more cheaply.

Time Line

1405 China opens new trade routes.

1455 Wars of the Roses in England begin.

1468 Songhai Empire founded in West Africa.

1480 Ivan III frees Moscow from Mongol rule, declaring himself as the Tsar of Russia.

1487 Bartholomeu Diaz sails round the southern tip of Africa.

1497 John Cabot sails from Bristol, England, and reaches Newfoundland.

1498 Columbus reaches the South American mainland.

1499-1502 Amerigo Vespucci explores the coast of South America. His name will be given to the entire American continent.

1513 The Portuguese reach Canton, China.

1517 Martin Luther rebels against the Church.

A date to remember
Columbus reaches America 1492

In August 1492 Christopher Columbus sailed west from Palos in Spain. The expedition of three ships and 120 men reached the Bahamas in October 1492 and were sure they had reached the Indies.

Don't look like the **Indies!** to me!

Important events

1438 In Peru the Inca ruler Pachacuti starts building his empire. The Incas grow potatoes and cotton and have advanced astronomical and surgical knowledge.

1453 Constantinople falls to the Ottomans. Byzantine Empire ends.

C.1455 Johannes Gutenberg produces his Bible in German (left). The first to be printed with movable type, it will sell over 40,000 copies by 1500.

1454 Francesco Foscari, doge (ruler) of Venice, signs treaty with the Ottomans.

1462 Lorenzo de Medici becomes ruler of Florence in Italy. Under him it becomes a centre of art and learning.

1477 Charles the Bold of Burgundy dies and the French take his lands.

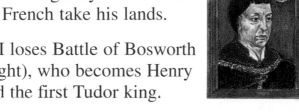

1485 Richard III loses Battle of Bosworth to Henry Tudor (right), who becomes Henry VII of England and the first Tudor king.

1498 Vasco da Gama (below) reaches India, the first European to do so.

1509 Henry VII dies and his son becomes King Henry VIII of England. Later, he will quarrel with the pope about a divorce.

Famous figures

Henry V of England (ruled 1413-22)
As part of the Hundred Years' War, Henry led successful campaigns in France and in 1415 defeated a much larger French army at Agincourt.

Henry VI of England (ruled 1422-61 and 1470-1)
Henry suffered from mental illness and his government was weak and unpopular.

Richard III of England (ruled 1483-5)
Brother of Edward IV, he was regent for his nephew the young Edward V. Edward and his younger brother (the Princes in the Tower) soon disappeared and Richard, who is said to have had them murdered, became king. He died at Bosworth Field fighting against Henry Tudor, who became Henry VII.

1520 to 1600
NATIONALISM V. RELIGION

The sixteenth century was dominated by religious struggles: between countries, between faiths, and even between different forms of Christianity. Martin Luther's challenge to the Catholic Church sent shock waves through Europe. It also coincided with a growing sense of nationalism. Many countries in north-western Europe, some ruled by Spain, adopted Luther's ideas challenging the church. In the Netherlands the movement for independence from their Spanish rulers and the Roman Catholic Church began to grow.

Far away in the Americas there were conflicts too. Local peoples had little chance against well-armed European explorers, who were increasingly coming as conquerors and missionaries.

A date to remember 1588
The Spanish Armada

*In the 1550s Britain was in religious turmoil: Protestant under Edward VI, Catholic under his successor, Mary I and Protestant under **her** successor, Elizabeth I. In 1588 Philip II of Spain sent the Armada to conquer Britain and make it Catholic again. It was defeated and wrecked by storms.*

You shouldn't have left Spain mate.

Time Line

1520 Henry VIII of England meets Francis I of France at the Field of the Cloth of Gold.

1521 Spaniard Hernan Cortes conquers the Aztec city of Tenochtitlán.

1523 Sweden becomes independent of Denmark.

1529 War between Catholics and Protestants in Switzerland.

1534 The Act of Supremacy cuts the link between Britain and Rome.

1571 In Sudan the Bornu Empire reaches its peak.

1572 The Spanish execute Topa Amaru, the last Inca ruler.

1582 Hideyoshi becomes leader in Japan.

1589 Protestant Henry of Navarre becomes Henry IV, king of Catholic France.

1598 The Edict of Nantes gives religious toleration to Protestants in France.

Important events

1520 Suleiman the Magnificent becomes ruler of the Ottoman Empire. His reign (until his death in 1566) is the empire's golden age.

1521 The Spanish explorer Hernan Cortes is the first European to meet the Aztecs.

C.1525 Babur invades India and becomes its first Mogul emperor. The Moguls build an empire of great wealth, encouraging art and learning.

1558 Elizabeth I comes to the throne. The daughter of Henry VIII and Anne Boleyn, she introduces a moderate Protestantism to Britain.

1568 Forced to abdicate, Mary, Queen of Scots flees to England. Put in prison and accused of plots against Elizabeth I, she is executed in 1587.

1571 A Christian fleet defeats a Turkish one at Lepanto, off Greece. Many of the ships are galleys (boats powered by rowers) and this is the last time they are used in battle.

1572 In France 20,000 Huguenots (French Protestants) are murdered in the St Batholomew's Day Massacre.

1588 Philip II of Spain, the most powerful ruler in Europe, and a Catholic, sends a fleet (the Armada) to attack Britain.

Famous figures

Ferdinand Magellan (c.1480-1521)
Magellan sailed west from Spain in 1519, around the tip of South America and into the Pacific (which he named). Although Magellan was killed in the Philippines, his fleet returned to Spain in 1522 – the first circumnavigation of the world.

Sir Francis Drake (c.1540-96)
English sailor and explorer, he was the first Englishman to sail around the world (1577-80). He helped defeat the Spanish Armada in 1588.

1600 to 1710
EXPLORING NEW WORLDS

By the seventeenth century the questioning spirit that led Luther to challenge the Catholic Church and the great navigators to sail beyond the horizon was firmly established. The northern (Calvinist) provinces of the Low Countries (now Holland) rebelled against their Spanish (Catholic) rulers, winning their independence in 1648. The sea voyages led to better navigation instruments. Together, the questioning attitude and technical advances produced an interest in the world and a huge growth in science. The Catholic Church had forbidden the study of the human body but by now scientists were ignoring this. William Harvey, an English physician, discovered how blood circulated around the body and published his findings in 1628.

Time Line

1602 Dutch traders arrive in Cambodia.

1605 Gunpowder Plot against James I of England.

1608 French explorer Samuel de Champlain founds Quebec.

1626 The Dutch buy the island of Manhattan from the Canarsee Indians.

1627 Shah Jehan becomes Mogul (Muslim) emperor of India.

1666 Most of London is destroyed in the Great Fire.

1680 The Portuguese found Sacramento in California.

1683 The Turks besiege Vienna.

1686 France annexes Madagascar.

1707 Union of England and Scotland.

1709 Afghans rebel against Persian rule and set up an independent state.

A date to remember 1626
Dutch purchase of Manhattan

My name is Peter Minuit, I am offering you goods to the value of sixty Dutch guilders to purchase the Island of Manhattan.

We are unfamiliar with the European practice of buying and selling land, we do not think of land as something that ccn be sold.

Important events

c.1600 Native Americans form the Iroquois League.

1607 English build Jamestown (left), their first settlement in North America.

1608 Hans Lippershey, a Dutch lens maker, builds the first telescope.

1609 German astronomer Johan Kepler descibes how the planets orbit the sun.

1618 Thirty Years' War begins in Germany. It will soon engulf most of Europe.

1620 The Pilgrim Fathers flee religious persecution in England, sailing to North America in the *Mayflower*.

1642 Civil war breaks out in England after years of distrust between Charles I and Parliament. The king is defeated and captured.

1649 Execution of Charles I.

1649 Oliver Cromwell, who led the opposition to Charles I, rules England as Lord Protector until he dies in 1658. His son, Richard, succeeds him, but is forced into exile in 1659. In 1660 Charles I's eldest son returns as King Charles II.

Famous figures

Akbar the Great of India (ruled 1542-1605)
Akbar expanded the Mongol empire of India. He encouraged art and science and abolished slavery.

Peter the Great of Russia (ruled 1682-1725)
Keen to modernise Russia, Peter passed laws against old customs, like having a beard.

Earl of Denbigh (1582-1643)
Unlike most Europeans he wore local clothes in India.

The front and back of a rupee made by English merchants in India in 1678.

TAX AND A TEA PARTY

Between 1756 and 1763 Britain fought in the Seven Years' War, which involved most European countries. By the end of the war Britain had taken France's territory in Canada and weakened its power in India, and was the greatest naval power in Europe. But wars are expensive, even for those who win, and Parliament increased taxes to pay for the war. This upset the American colonists. Although they had no members of Parliament to represent them, they still had to pay the taxes. They began a protest with the slogan 'No taxation without representation'. In 1773 tea was taxed. When British ships arrived in Boston Harbour with a cargo of tea, protestors boarded the ships and threw the tea overboard.

A date to remember 1773
The Boston Tea Party

Time Line

1718 The French found New Orleans.

1720 China conquers Tibet.

1728 Danish navigator Vitus Bering explores the strait named after him.

1755 An earthquake in Lisbon kills 30,000 people.

1756 The ruler of Bengal puts 146 British people in a tiny prison – the Black Hole of Calcutta. Many die.

1759 Britain takes Quebec from the French.

1767 The Burmese invade Siam (Thailand).

1768 War between Russia and Turkey.

1770 The Boston Massacre: British troops fire on a crowd protesting about taxes.

1773 Peasant uprising in Russia.

c.1775 The Masai extend their power in East Africa.

Important events   Famous figures

1725 Peter the Great of Russia dies. One of Russia's greatest rulers, he increased the size and strength of the country and introduced new industries.

1727 J. S. Bach composes the St Matthew Passion. (Some historians think the date is 1729).

1734 German physician M. Fuchs invents the fire extinguisher.

1715 & 1745 Unsuccessful revolts by Scottish Jacobites (supporters of James II and his descendants) against the Hanoverian kings of England.

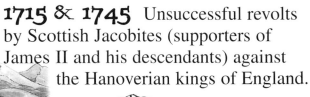

1740 Frederick the Great (right) becomes king of Prussia. He leads his country in many wars, and when he dies in 1786 Prussia is twice as big as it was in 1740.

1757 The sextant is invented. It is an enormous help to navigation.

C.1760 Slaves from Africa are sold at auction when they reach the Caribbean and North America.

1760 George III becomes king of Britain. During his reign Britain loses the War of American Independence and the colonies get their independence in 1783.

James Cook (1728-79)

A great navigator and explorer, Cook made three epic voyages.
<u>First voyage 1768-71</u>: He charted the coasts of New Zealand and New Guinea, explored the east coast of Australia, and claimed it for Britain.
<u>Second voyage 1772-5</u>: Cook sailed around Antarctica. Strict about his crew's diet and hygiene, only one of his men died.
<u>Third voyage 1776-80</u>: trying to find a route round the north of America, Cook was killed in Hawaii.

Dr James Lind (1716-94)

The naval surgeon James Lind realised that scurvy, which plagued ships' crews, was due to lack of Vitamin C.

1775 to 1800
REVOLUTION!

In the reign of Louis XIV (1643-1715) France was one of the richest and most powerful countries in Europe. Since then, however, weak kings and corrupt ministers had caused decline abroad and growing unrest at home. In May 1789, faced by huge debts, Louis XVI called a meeting of the Estates-General (a sort of parliament) – its first meeting since 1614! The meeting was attended by representatives of the clergy, nobility and commoners. In June the commoners broke away to form their own National Assembly. This really marks the start of the French Revolution. The commoners, ignored and despised by the clergy and nobility, had never acted independently before.

A date to remember 1789
The French Revolution

The chopper is called a guillotine, it's named after Joseph Ignace Guillotin who thought it would be a quick way to die.

Most of the French revolutionaries' victims were executed by having their heads cut off with a guillotine. It was named after Joseph Ignace Guillotin, the French doctor and revolutionary, who recommended its use in this way.

Time Line

1780 Peruvian Indians rebel against Spanish rule.

1780 The Gordon Riots in London.

1787 Famine and rice riots in Edo, Japan.

1788 England transports first convicts to Australia.

1789 French Revolution begins.

1789 George Washington becomes first President of the United States.

1791-2 War between China and Tibet.

1791 Canada is divided into English or French-speaking areas.

1792 Denmark bans the slave trade, the first country to do so.

1793-4 The Reign of Terror in France.

1798 Nelson defeats the French Navy at the Battle of the Nile.

40

Important events

1776 On 4 July leaders of the American colonies declare their independence from Britain.

1778 Captain Cook's ships *Resolution* and *Discovery* moored off the north-west coast of Canada (right) during his third voyage. The voyage is a failure. He does not find the route round the north of America (it was iced over) and he was killed in Hawaii the following year.

1781 Helped by France and Spain, the American rebels defeat the British at Yorktown. The British then surrender.

1793 Alexander Mackenzie, a young Scottish merchant, explores the Canadian interior.

1799 Napoleon Bonaparte makes himself First Consul of France. It is really a coup d'etat against the leaders of the revolutionary government who were no good at governing. They quarrelled among themselves and some were even sent to the guillotine.

Famous figures

George Washington (1st US President 1789-97)
His military skill helped win the American War of Independence. He chaired the committee that drew up the American Constitution and was president twice.

Marie Antoinette (1755-93)
She became queen of France when she married Louis XVI in 1770. Extravagant and so unpopular, she was executed in 1793.

King Louis XVI of France (ruled 1774-92)
Although he made a few reforms in an attempt to stave off the French Revolution, they were not enough. He and his family tried to flee Paris in 1791, but were captured and imprisoned. Louis was sent to the guillotine in 1792.

REVOLUTIONARY WARS

Under Napoleon, the French again dominated Europe, just as they had in the reign of Louis XIV (1643-1715). A brilliant general and administrator, by 1807 Napoleon had built an empire stretching from the River Elbe in the north, south through Italy to Naples, where he made his brother king. He then attacked Spain and Portugal. In fact he was too successful, because it made the rulers of countries he had not yet attacked, like Britain, Sweden and Russia, unite against him.

Revolutionary struggles were not just going on in Europe. In South America the Spanish and Portuguese colonies were declaring themselves independent. And the Boers (Dutch settlers) in South Africa set out on the Great Trek in 1835 to escape British control.

A date to remember
1815 Napoleon defeated at Waterloo

Time Line

1801 Russia annexes Georgia.

1802 Siam (Thailand) annexes Cambodia.

1804 Serbs rebel against Turkish rule.

1808 Importing of slaves into USA banned.

1816 Argentina gets independence from Spain.

1818 Chile becomes independent.

1821 Beginning of Greek struggle for independence from Turkey.

1824 Mexico becomes an independent republic.

1825 Indonesians revolt against the Dutch in Java.

1847 Liberia, the colony for freed slaves set up by the US in West Africa, becomes independent.

1848 Karl Marx and Friedrich Engels publish the *Communist Manifesto*.

Important events

c.1800 Napoleon's invasion of Egypt in 1798 led to European interest in its ancient history.

1805 The Battle of Trafalgar: the French navy is defeated by the English led by Nelson.

1812 Napoleon attacks Russia. The Russians retreat and destroy everything. Winter sets in and forces the French to retreat. Thousands of Napoleon's soldiers die.

1815 After defeating Napoleon at Waterloo, his captors exile him to the small island of St Helena in the South Atlantic. He dies there in 1821.

1819 The Peterloo Massacre: in Manchester a peaceful crowd calling for political reform is charged by local militia. Eleven people die and hundreds are injured.

1837 Victoria becomes Queen of Great Britain and Ireland. Despite many revolutions in Europe, she retains her throne until her death in 1901.

1848 'The Year of Revolutions' in Europe, from Poland in the north to Sicily in the south. But only in France was a government overthrown.

Famous figures

Duke of Wellington (1769-1852)
Best known for his victory at Waterloo, Wellington became British prime minister twice.

George IV (reigned 1820-30)
In 1810 he became Prince Regent (and king in all but name), because of his father, George III's madness.

William IV (reigned 1830-7)
The brother of George IV, William was called 'the Sailor King' because of his service in the Royal Navy. He had no children and his niece Victoria succeeded him.

CROSSING CONTINENTS

I n 1860 thousands of workers flocked to the United States looking for work on the country's biggest construction project: the Union Pacific transcontinental railroad. It was designed to stretch across two-thirds of the United States, spanning a distance of 2,776 km. Each rail was 9 m long and weighed a hefty 255 kg – it took four men to lift each one. Living conditions were harsh and basic, and diseases like smallpox would spread quickly among the workers, many of whom came from Ireland and even as far as China. Finally, on 10 May, 1869, the Union Pacific track was completed.

Time Line

1853 US sends gunboats to force Japan to open its ports to foreign trade.

1855 In Africa, the explorer David Livingstone discovers the Victoria Falls.

1857 Indian troops mutiny against the British.

1859 Oil discovered in US state of Pennsylvania.

1860 Robert Burke and William Wills set out to cross Australia.

1865 American Civil War ends, but the defeated South remains very bitter.

1871 William I of Prussia becomes Kaiser (emperor) of a united Germany.

1874 Henry Stanley sets out to explore the Congo.

1884 The French annexe Cambodia.

1893 New Zealand is the first country to let women vote.

A date to remember
East meets West
1869

The Union Pacific track, laid westwards from Nebraska, meets the Central Pacific track, laid eastwards from California, at Promontory Summit, Utah. It was now possible to travel right across the US by rail.

Important events

c.1850s Explorers, farmers and goldminers make the long trek to the Wild West, hoping to make their fortunes.

1861 Abraham Lincoln becomes 16th president of the United States. He wants to end slavery. In the Civil War he helps the northern states defeat the south, which wants to keep slavery.

1866 Scottish missionary and explorer David Livingstone returns to Africa for a third time, to seek out the source of the River Nile.

1876 Queen Victoria (seated left) becomes Empress of India.

1879 The first war between Britain and the Zulu kingdom in South Africa begins.

1880-1 The First Anglo-Boer War begins.

1882 In Geneva the first successful blood transfusion is given to a woman after childbirth.

1890 Native American Chief, Big Foot, dies in the Battle of Wounded Knee.

1894 Rudyard Kipling writes *The Jungle Book*, about an Indian boy raised by wolves in the jungle.

1895 In Paris the Lumière brothers give the world's first film show – only 35 people turn up!

1896 The first modern Olympic Games are held in Athens as a tribute to the Games' Ancient Greek origins.

Famous figures

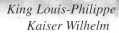

King Louis-Philippe of France (ruled 1830-48)
Louis-Philippe sided with the people during the French Revolution. His own government was overthrown in 1848 and he died in exile in England in 1850.

Kaiser Wilhelm of Germany (ruled 1888-1918)
Wilhelm's aggressive foreign policy contributed to the First World War. When Germany was defeated in 1918 US President Wilson refused to negotiate peace if he stayed in power. Wilhelm abdicated and went to The Netherlands. He died there in 1941.

Benjamin Disraeli (1804-81)
Disraeli was a novelist and a Conservative politician. He was prime minister of Britain in 1868, and from 1874-1880.

Karl Marx (1818-83)
Joint author of the *Communist Manifesto*, which called for new states with communist governments.

45

ICEBERGS AND ICE CAPS

By the beginning of the twentieth century most of the Earth's land surface had been explored. The polar regions were the only large areas that remained unexplored. It soon became a matter of personal and national pride to be the first expedition to reach the North and South Poles.

As well as the polar regions and ocean depths (for which there was not yet the technology), there was one other area awaiting exploration: the air. And in the USA the Wright brothers, with their dream of powered flight, were on their way to making this possible. On 17 December, 1903 their first powered aircraft, the *Flyer*, with a wingspan of 12.3 m, flew 36 m and stayed in the air for 12 seconds. Their dream had come true!

A date to remember 1912
Titanic sinks

In 1912, the Titanic, *the world's largest ship, was launched. Amid much publicity the liner sailed for America, but struck an iceberg in the North Atlantic. It sank and 1490 people died.*

Time Line

1900 In China the Boxer Rebellion against foreign influence is crushed by an international force.

1901 Queen Victoria dies.

1901 The Commonwealth of Australia is established.

1905 Norway becomes independent of Sweden.

1905 Revolt in St Petersburg crushed by the Tsar's troops.

1905 The Japanese destroy a Russian fleet at Tsushima.

1909 The Sultan of Turkey is overthrown by a group of nationalists.

1910 The King of Portugal is overthrown.

1911 Chinese Revolution begins.

1912 Libya comes under Italian control.

1912 Henry Ford begins mass-producing cars.

Important events

1903 The Wright Brothers, Orville and Wilbur, prove that man can fly. Their aircraft, the *Flyer*, stays airborne for just 12 seconds on its first flight.

1906 The guns of Britain's largest battleship, HMS *Dreadnought,* fire shells 30.4 cm in diameter. The ship's five twin–gun turrets can fire in all directions.

1911 Norwegian Roald Amundsen reaches the South Pole a month before British naval officer, Captain Robert Scott. Amundsen and his team dressed like the Inuits against the cold.

1912–13 Growing nationalism in the Balkans leads to two short wars. This unrest will lead to the murder of Archduke Franz Ferdinand, heir to the Austrian throne, on a visit to Sarajevo in 1914 and from that murder came the First World War.

Famous figures

Captain Robert Scott (1869-1912)
Scott led scientific trips in Antarctica. He wanted to be the first to reach the South Pole but was beaten by Roald Amundsen. Trapped in bad weather, Scott and his team died of exhaustion and cold.

Ernest Shackleton (1874-1922)
Shackleton led teams of explorers to the Antarctic and is best known for his 1914 trip, an epic test of endurance when his ship was crushed by ice. He survived this and went on to later expeditions.

Robert Peary (1856-1920)
An American naval officer, Peary claimed to have reached the North Pole with five companions in 1909 on his eighth attempt. Some people doubted his story, saying it would have been impossible to trek over rough ice for 61 km a day in Arctic weather.

1914 to 1927
WAR - AND PEACE?

After the assassination of the heir to the Austrian throne in 1914, Europe was engulfed by war. On one side an increasingly powerful united Germany was in alliance with the old-established Austrio-Hungarian Empire, which was made up of different countries becoming restive under foreign rule. Facing these allies were France, Russia and Britain. The war was really about European issues, but most countries involved had overseas colonies, so troops from all over the world fought in the war. In September 1914 British politicians confidently said the war would be 'over by Christmas'. It was not. It ended just over four years later, in November 1918. The death toll had been so great that people hoped the First World War would be 'the war to end all wars'.

A date to remember 1918
Armistice Day

Time Line

28 July 1914 Austria declares war on Serbia.

March 1917 Tsar Nicholas II of Russia abdicates.

April 1917 USA enters war, supporting Britain and her allies.

1918 Spanish flu pandemic begins. Millions will die.

1919 The Peace of Versailles. The terms were so hard on Germany that in 20 years' time war would break out again.

1919 League of Nations founded to help keep world peace.

1920 USA refuses to join League of Nations.

1921 Mao Zedong and Li Ta-chao form Chinese communist party.

1922 Atatürk seizes power in Turkey.

1927 Canberra becomes capital of Australia.

Important events

1914 On a visit to Sarajevo the royal chauffeur took a wrong turn, so Gavrilo Princip had a second chance to kill the Archduke Franz Ferdinand and his wife. This time he succeeded.

1915 In Belgium and northern France (the Western Front) the two sides dig in, each trying to take a few metres of land from the other.

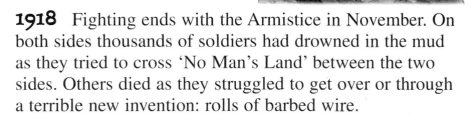

1917 Tsar of Russia is overthrown and a democratic government is set up. It soon fails.

1918 Fighting ends with the Armistice in November. On both sides thousands of soldiers had drowned in the mud as they tried to cross 'No Man's Land' between the two sides. Others died as they struggled to get over or through a terrible new invention: rolls of barbed wire.

1918 After many years of campaigning, women in Britain over the age of 30 are allowed to vote.

1919 The Peace Treaty of Versailles made Germany give up land and pay huge sums of reparations (compensation).

1921 After several years of nationalist unrest, David Lloyd George, the prime minister of Britain, agrees to the formation of the Irish Free State (Eire) within the British Empire.

Famous figures

Tsar Nicholas II and his family (murdered 1918)
Russian tsars were absolute rulers. As other European countries became democratic, unrest in Russia grew. The First World War was the final straw. The communists took over, imprisoning and then murdering the Tsar and his family.

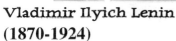

Vladimir Ilyich Lenin (1870-1924)
Lenin became leader of the communist government that replaced the tsar in 1918.

Josef Stalin (1879-1953)
By 1927 Stalin had taken over power from Lenin. Quite ruthless, millions of Russians died as a result of his policies.

1928 to 1940
PEACE FOR OUR TIME?

The effects of the First World War lasted long after it ended. First, the war had cost every country that took part a huge amount. Second, around the world the prices of raw materials and agricultural goods slumped. This hit the producer countries, like Germany and Australia, extremely hard, causing poverty and mass unemployment. Third, America's economy was weak, so every country that depended on exporting goods to the US (and most did) lost its best market. Then, in October 1929, the New York stock exchange crashed, triggering the Great Depression. Around the world people struggled to live on lower (or no) wages, which meant governments had less income from tax. As a result, political unrest grew in many countries.

A date to remember 1939
War is declared

Time Line

1928   Chiang Kai-shek is President of China.

1929   In India Gandhi begins his campaign to win independence from Britain.

1932   Under Adolf Hitler the German Nazi party makes big election gains.

1934   The Long March of Chinese communists under Mao Zedong begins.

1935   Italy invades Ethiopia using poison gas.

1936   Spanish Civil War begins. (Lasts until 1939.)

1936   In England Edward VIII abdicates.

1937   Japan's attack on China leads to war.

1938   Nazi plots in Chile and Brazil fail.

1938   Desperate to avoid another war, Prime Minister Neville Chamberlain claims to have negotiated 'peace for our time' with Hitler. He has not and war is declared in 1939.

Important events

1928 Stalin imposes state control of agriculture. All resistance is crushed and millions starve to death.

1929 Chicago gangster, Al Capone, orders the murder of seven rivals on 14 February – St Valentine's Day.

1932 Bonnie Parker and Clyde Barrow begin their crime spree. They will be shot dead in 1934.

1936 Benito Mussolini, Italy's fascist dictator, supports General Franco (a fascist) in his civil war against the republicans in Spain.

1936 Adolf Hitler sends troops into the Rhineland in defiance of the Peace Treaty of Versailles. This is a challenge to other European leaders.

1939 All through the 1930s Hitler builds up German power. Finally, on 1 September, he orders the invasion of Poland. Two days later France and Britain declare war on Germany and another war begins.

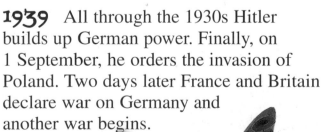

1940 The British RAF won the Battle of Britain against the German *Luftwaffe*, but there were heavy losses of planes and pilots on both sides.

Famous figures

Franciso Franco (ruled 1939-75)
Leader of the nationalists in the Spanish Civil War, he became dictator in 1939 on the defeat of the republicans.

Adolf Hitler (ruled 1933-45)
A charismatic leader but bad general, he committed suicide.

Winston Churchill (1874-1965)
Prime Minister of Britain who announced German surrender in 1945.

Franklin D. Roosevelt (1882-1945)
32nd President of the USA (1933-45), his New Deal in 1933 helped end the Great Depression. The Japanese attack on Pearl Harbor in 1941 brought the US into the war against Germany. He died three weeks before it ended.

1940 to 1955
A SECOND WORLD WAR

Germany had been preparing for war for some years, increasing its army, navy and air force, and building factories to make the weapons these forces needed. In the first three years of the war this preparation paid off, for Germany and her allies had the upper hand. The British were unprepared for war, and the retreat of their ill-prepared force from Dunkirk in 1940 was a disaster. But very slowly things began to change. Despite a non-aggression treaty with Russia, Hitler invaded that country in 1941, easing the pressure on British forces in the west. When Japan (an ally of German) attacked the US base of Pearl Harbor in December 1941, the US entered the war against them.

Time Line

1942 Britain and its allies defeat German forces at El Alamein in North Africa.

1943 Russians defeat Germans at Stalingrad.

1945 Roosevelt dies. Harry Truman becomes the US president.

1947 India becomes independent and is divided into Hindu India and Muslim Pakistan.

1949 Siam is renamed Thailand.

1952 King Farouk of Egypt abdicates.

1953 Mount Everest climbed by Edmund Hilary and Sherpa Tenzing.

1954 Vietnam War begins.

1955 President Perón overthrown in Argentina.

A date to remember 1945
Hiroshima bombed

In August 1945, America dropped atomic bombs on the Japanese cities of Hiroshima and Nagasaki, killing tens of thousands of people. The bombing effectively ended Japanese involvement in the war

Important events

1944 D-Day (6 June) as the Allies start to drive the Germans out of France.

1945 Trials of senior Nazis for war crimes begin at Nuremberg (top). The crimes include the murder of millions of Jews and other European minorities.

1945 Peace talks between President Truman, Stalin and Clement Attlee, the British Prime Minister.

1945 United Nations founded.

1948 Cold War begins.

1948 Russia blockades West Berlin to force the Western Powers to let it become part of communist East Germany. Supplies are airlifted to the city.

1950-3 The Korean War. When it ends Korea is divided into two countries: North and South Korea.

Famous figures

General Charles de Gaulle (1890-1970)
French leader who organised resistance to the Germans and became President of France (1959-69).

Mahatma Gandhi (1869-1948)
An Indian nationalist, Gandhi followed a policy of non-violent civil disobedience in a campaign to win India's independence from British rule. This is achieved in 1947, but in 1948 he is killed by a Hindu fanatic who objected to the creation of Pakistan.

Eva (Evita) Perón (1919-52)
The second wife of Juan Perón, President of Argentina, and unofficial Minister of Health and Labour. Her social reforms made her popular among the poor.

1955 to 1970
THE RACE TO THE MOON

The Moon has fascinated people for as long as there has been anyone to look at it – its appearance in so many myths, legends and religions shows that. People dreamed of travelling to it, but only in the late twentieth century did that become possible. Even then it might not have happened without the Cold War.

After the Second World War two superpowers emerged to dominate the world: the USA and the USSR (Union of Soviet Socialist Republics). They represented two completely opposite political systems: capitalism and democracy versus totalitarian communism. They did not fight each other directly, but each country strove to prove its system was best. And the space race was crucial in this trial of strength.

A date to remember 1969
Man walks on the moon

Space travel only became possible because of the rocket technology developed by German scientists during the Second World War. Before that, no flying machine could produce enough energy to get a spacecraft through the Earth's gravitational field. The space race was hugely expensive.

Time Line

1956   President Nasser of Egypt nationalises the Suez Canal.

1956   The USSR brutally crushes an anti-communist uprising in Hungary.

1957   The first space flight: the USSR's satellite, *Sputnik I*, orbits the Earth.

1958   Texas Instruments patents the silicon chip.

1960   Sharpeville Massacre: 67 black South African protesters shot by government troops.

1960   China and India fight over border claims.

1961   Berlin Wall built by communist East Germany to stop its citizens fleeing to the capitalist West.

1968   USSR crushes the Prague Spring, a liberal movement in Czechslovakia.

1969   US astronaut Neil Armstrong becomes the first person to reach and walk on the Moon.

Important events

1956 Elvis Presley's *Blue Suede Shoes* tops the charts.

1961 USSR cosmonaut Yuri Gagarin is first person to make a space flight.

1962 The Beatles' first single *Love Me Do*.

1965 In June US astronaut Edward White makes the first space walk.

1966 Mao Zedong starts Cultural Revolution in China. Thousands will die in the ten-year terror.

1967 Civil war in Nigeria: the Ibo seek independence. Nigerian government uses

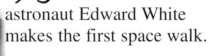

genocide against the Ibo to take back their breakaway state of Biafra in 1970.

1967 Six Days' War between Israel and the Arab states.

1968 Rioting and brutal atrocities in Northern Ireland.

1968 The USA have half a million troops in Vietnam, but will loose the war.

Famous figures

Fidel Castro (born 1927)
Communist head of state in Cuba since 1958. In 1961 lets USSR install nuclear missiles.

John F Kennedy (1917-63)
In 1961 says US will land a man on the Moon by 1970. Tells USSR to get missiles out of Cuba.

Martin Luther King (1929-68)
Leading civil rights leader in US.

Nikita Khruschev (1894-1971)
First Secretary of the Communist Party after Stalin's death and the first to denounce his policies. Head of state during Cuban Missile Crisis. By removing the missiles from Cuba he avoided war with the US.

1970 to 1980
CHANGING REGIMES

Just because there are no major conflicts it doesn't mean the world is at peace, as the Seventies demonstrate. All over the world there were conflicts as countries tried to grab more territory (the Iran-Iraq War) or change the regime governing them (the USSR's invasion of Afghanistan).

Some changes were more peaceful. In the USA Nixon resigned because of scandal. And after the Spanish dictator General Franco died, his successor, Juan Carlos, brought back democracy in 1977.

The pop music of the Seventies reflected the unsettled time. The Beatles remained popular, but their fresh image was replaced by the Rolling Stones, the anarchy of Punk and the songs of Jimi Hendrix.

A date to remember 1976
First Concorde flight

Whooooo!

Time Line

1970 Khmer Republic set up in Cambodia.

1970 Israel and Egypt fight over Sinai.

1971 Pakistan attacks India, but is defeated.

1973 In Chile the US supports overthrow of Marxist President Allende.

1973 Yom Kippur War between Israel and Egypt.

1973 American troops finally leave Vietnam.

1974 Revolution in Portugal.

1974 Emperor Haile Selassie of Ethiopia is deposed by Marxists.

1979 The left-wing Sandanistas take power in a coup in Nicaragua.

1980 Rhodesia becomes independent of Britain and is renamed Zimbabwe.

1980 Death of President Tito, ruler of Yugoslavia since 1945.

Important events

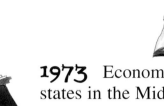

1973 Economic crisis as oil-producing states in the Middle East reduce output.

1974 Watergate scandal: US President Nixon allows illegal bugging. He resigns.

1976 Pol Pot, communist leader of Cambodia, orders brutal regime to reconstruct country. Millions die.

1979 Saddam Hussein makes himself president, prime minister and head of the armed forces of Iraq.

1979 The shah of Iran (left) is overthrown and an Islamic republic declared by Ayatollah Khomeini (right). In 1980 Iran and Iraq begin a bitter war which ends in 1988.

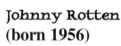

1979 Civil war begins in Afghanistan. The USSR sends troops in support of the government. This provokes a guerrilla war against the Soviet forces.

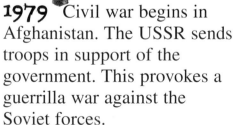

1980 In Poland there is serious unrest in the shipyards as Solidarity, the independent trade union movement led by Lech Walesa, gains more and more support. The communist government bans it.

Famous figures

Jimi Hendrix (1942-70) Brilliant and flamboyant American rock guitarist and singer.

Mick Jagger (born 1943) English rock singer and song-writer who founded the Rolling Stones with guitarist Keith Richards c.1962.

Johnny Rotten (born 1956) Lead singer of one of the most popular punk bands, the Sex Pistols. Punk was a particularly anarchic type of music, which began as a form of protest. Its followers' spiky hair and safety pins soon became a uniform.

THE END OF COMMUNISM

L ooking back over the past, every period seems full of great changes. But centuries ago, when roads hardly existed and the fastest transport for most people was walking pace, wars and revolutions could sweep across a country and leave most people's lives unchanged. The communication revolution in all its forms changed that. During the years 1981 to 1993 the people of the countries under Russian control became increasingly aware of the differences between their lives under communism and the lives of their neighbours in the capitalist West. Radio and television, which communist governments tried to control, played a vital part in this.

Time Line

1983 Democracy restored in Argentina.

1984 Long drought in Sudan, Ethiopia and Chad. Thousands die of starvation.

1984 Britain and China agree terms for Hong Kong's independence.

1985 In South Africa black people riot against apartheid system.

1986 US bombs Libya in revenge for terrorist attacks in Europe.

1986 Chernobyl nuclear reactor disaster in USSR. Nuclear fall-out affects northern Europe and Asia.

1989 Chinese authorities order crushing of peaceful pro-reform protests in Tiananmen Square, Peking. Several thousand die.

1993 World Trade Center, New York, bombed. Five people killed.

1993 In Russia, head of state Boris Yeltsin crushes rebellion by communists.

A date to remember
1989
Fall of the Berlin Wall

The heavily fortified Berlin Wall was the greatest symbol of the Cold War division between East and West. In November 1989 the government of East Germany collapsed and so did the Wall. The communist era was finally over.

Important events

1985 'Live Aid', huge fundraising concerts for African famine relief are held in the UK and USA. Performers include David Bowie, Paul McCartney and Bob Geldof.

1985 Presidents Reagan of the USA and Gorbachev of the USSR hold meetings in Geneva, Switzerland.

1989 Hirohito, Emperor of Japan since 1926, dies. Regarded by his people as a divine being, he was forced to become a constitutional ruler after Japan's surrender in 1945.

1990 Margaret Thatcher, Britain's first woman Prime Minister, resigns after holding that office for eleven years.

1991 President Gorbachev resigns and Boris Yeltsin (right) becomes head of a federation of independent states (the CIS). The USSR ceases to exist.

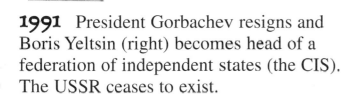

1991 End of apartheid in South Africa, a triumph for reformers like Nelson Mandela.

1991 Civil war among the republics of former Yugolavia. Slovenia and Croatia have democratic governments and want independence. Serbia, which is stronger, will not agree.

1991 The Gulf War. An international force under the United Nations forces the Iraqi army to withdraw from Kuwait which they had invaded in 1990.

Famous figures

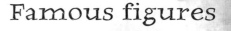

Anwar Sadat (1918-81)
President of Egypt from 1970, he sought peace in the Middle East, sharing the 1978 Nobel Peace Prize with Israel's Menachem Begin. He was shot by a Muslim extremist.

Colonel Gaddafi (born 1942)
Libya's head of state since 1970. For years ostracised by most countries because of his support for terrrorism, he has softened his stance in recent years to get the economic blockade of his country lifted.

Yasser Arafat (1929-2004)
Leader of the Palestinian Liberation Organisation from 1968, he became Palestinian President in 1996. He shared the 1994 Nobel Peace Prize with Israelis Yitzhak Rabin and Shimon Peres for the peace accord with Israel. After Rabin's murder by a Jewish extremist in 1995, Arafat was largely ignored by the USA and Israel.

1995 to ?
A FUTURE IN SPACE?

It is a cliché to say the world has shrunk, but like most such sayings it has some truth. In the nineteenth century when railways were the newest form of transport people could, for the first time, visit places without the need for an uncomfortable stagecoach journey. So, if you could afford it, a town 50 kilometres away was no longer as foreign as a distant country. Then came the internal combustion engine which, in the form of cars and trucks, gave a supremely flexible, independent form of transport for people and goods. Now, with only the deepest parts of the oceans left to explore, people are looking beyond the Earth. Will space travel really develop so that one day it will bring the distant planets as close as the railways once brought towns and cities?

A **date** to remember

9/11 2001

Time Line

1995 Thousands die as a massive earthquake hits the Japanese city of Kobe.

1995 Murder of Israeli prime minister Yitzhak Rabin by a Jewish extremist.

1995 In Rwanda Tutsi troops murder thousands of Hutu refugees.

1996 Taliban religious extremists take control of Afghanistan.

1997 Mars *Pathfinder* probe and *Sojourner* rover explore surface of Mars.

2001 The twin towers of the World Trade Center in New York are destroyed when two airliners, hijacked by Islamic extremists, are flown into them. A third plane is crashed into the Pentagon in Washington.

2004 George W. Bush makes Condoleezza Rice his Secretary of State to deal with foreign affairs, the first black woman to hold such a senior post.

Important events

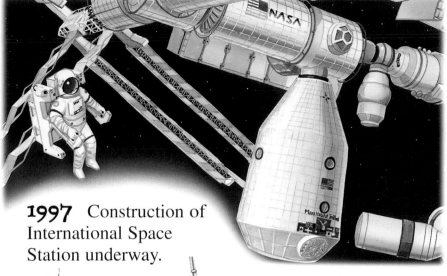

1997 Construction of International Space Station underway.

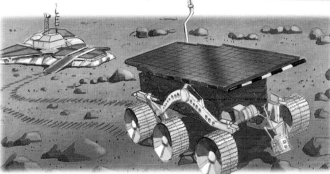

1997 Mars *Pathfinder* successfully explores that planet's surface.

2001 American President George W. Bush declares war on terror. In a speech, he describes Iran, Iraq and North Korea as forming an 'axis of evil'. This causes anger in the three countries and anxiety among moderate states.

2003 George W. Bush orders the invasion of Iraq, claiming its leader Saddam Hussein has WMDs (weapons of mass destruction). This view is shared by his ally, Tony Blair, prime minister of Britain. No WMDs are found.

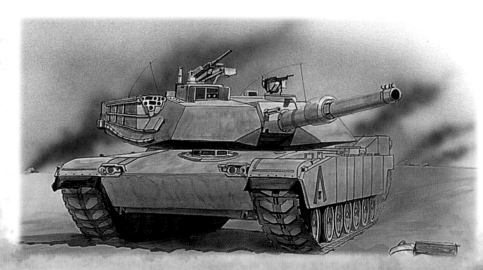

Famous figures

Diana, Princess of Wales (1961-97)
The former wife of Prince Charles, heir to the British throne, she died in a car crash in Paris. Their sons are Princes William and Harry.

Robert Mugabe (born 1924)
President of Zimbabwe since 1987, he has turned it into a one-party state. His land reforms – turning farmers and their workers off their land and giving it to his supporters – has led the once-rich food-exporting country to import much of its food.

Nelson Mandela (born 1918)
Activist for the rights of black people in South Africa, he was imprisoned in 1964. Released in 1990, he helped negotiate the end of apartheid and became South Africa's first democratically elected black president in 1994.

Glossary

abdicate when a ruler gives up his or her throne and the right to rule.

annexe take over territory belonging to another country, usually illegally.

apartheid system of government in South Africa which segregated (kept apart) black and white people. It ended in 1991.

astronaut English and American name for a person trained for space travel.

astronomy study of the stars and galaxies of outer space.

archaeologist someone who studies human history through the remains of what earlier people have left.

Buddhist follower of the teachings of the Indian philosopher Siddhartha Gautama (died 496 BC).

Byzantine the society and empire that flourished around Byzantium (modern Istanbul, Turkey) AD 610 to 1453.

colony settlement set up by people of one country, under their own laws, in another land.

constitution rules by which a country is run. A constitution can be a set of laws (eg USA) or a collection of unwritten traditions (eg UK).

coup d'etat sudden, illegal, and usually violent, seizing of power from a government. Also called a coup.

cosmonaut Russian term for astronaut.

Crusades wars between Christian and Muslim armies fought between 1095 and 1291, over the right to control the sacred sites in the Holy Land.

Cultural Revolution movement started in 1966 by communist leader Mao Zedong to destroy every trace of tradition in China. It ended in 1976.

dynasty line of rulers who are related, such as a father and son.

exile someone sent to live far from their home, usually as a punishment.

genocide deliberate, systematic killing of one race of people by another.

Goths Germanic peoples who invaded the Roman Empire. Then Ostrogoths (eastern Goths) founded a kingdom in Italy and Visigoths (western Goths) founded another in Spain.

Hanoverian dynasty of British kings, originally from Germany, who ruled from 1741 to 1901.

Holy Land now part of Israel and Palestine, to Christians it is where Christ lived. It is also sacred to Jews and Muslims.

Holy Roman Empire created by the popes to unite western Europe. In 800 Charlemagne became its first emperor.

Homo erectus early man who first walked upright on two feet.

Homo sapiens sapiens scientific name for modern man.

Huns warlike nomads from Central Asia who attacked Europe during the fourth and fifth centuries AD.

hunter-gatherers people who live by hunting and collecting wild food.

internal combustion engine engine burning fuel in a cylinder and not in an external firebox as a steam engine does.

Islam religion founded by the prophet Mohammed c.630.

Jacobites Scottish political group that opposed the Hanoverians.

leper someone suffering from leprosy.

Linear A writing used in Crete c.1700 to 1450 BC and still not completely understood.

Linear B writing used in Crete c.1400 to 1200. It has been deciphered.

megalith large stone forming part of an ancient monument.

Mongols nomadic people who lived in Central Asia.

Moors Muslim people from north-west Africa who ruled the Spanish Peninsula from c.710 to1492.

Moguls dynasty of Indian rulers (1526 to 1857) whose ancestors had been Mongols.

Muslim follower of Islam.

nationalist someone who wants independence for his or her country.

nomads people with no settled home who travel around to find pasture for their animals and food for themselves.

Ottoman dynasty of Turkish rulers who were powerful from the fifteenth to the nineteenth centuries. The word also describes the empire they ruled.

Pharaoh Ancient Egyptian ruler.

plague infectious and often deadly disease spread by rat fleas. Its medical name is 'bubonic plague'.

regime a government, usually a dictatorial one.

scribe someone who writes letters and keeps records, usually in societies where few people can read or write.

scurvy disease caused by lack of vitamin C. It was common among sailors who had no fresh fruit and vegetables on long voyages.

sextant navigation instrument using the planets to work out direction.

shaduf weighted pole to lift water.

Soviet belonging to the former USSR.

stylus pointed writing tool.

USSR (Union of Soviet Socialist Republics) communist states once ruled as a huge unit with Moscow as the capital.

Vandals fierce Germanic peoples who attacked Spain, France and Italy c.455 BC, causing great destruction – which is why we still use the term.

Index

61

Published in Great Britain in 2005 by
Book House, an imprint of
The Salariya Book Company Ltd
25 Marlborough Place
Brighton BN1 1UB

Please visit the Salariya Book Company at:
www.salariya.com

ISBN 1 904642 57-8

A catalogue record for this book is available from the British Library.
Printed and bound in China.
The Salariya Book Company operates an environmentally friendly policy wherever possible

Editors: Michael Ford, Claire Andrews
Illustrated by David Antram, Mark Peppé, John James, Mark Bergin, Carolyn Scrace

Visit our website at **www.book-house.co.uk**
for free electronic versions of:
You wouldn't want to be an Egyptian Mummy!
You wouldn't want to be a Roman Gladiator!
Avoid joining Shackleton's Polar Expedition!

HABSBURG EMPERORS (cont)

9 Ferdinand II (1619-1637)
10 Ferdinand III
   (1637-1657)
11 Leopold I (1658-1705)
12 Joseph I (1705-1711)
13 Charles VI (1711-1740)
14 Charles VII of Bavaria
   (1742-1745)

HABSBURG - LORRAINE EMPERORS

1 Francis I of Lorraine
   (1745-1765)
2 Joseph II (1765-1790)
3 Leopold II (1790-1792)
4 Francis II (1792-1806)

TSARS, EMPERORS AND GRAND PRINCES OF RUSSIA

1 Dmitri Donskoi
   (1359-1389)
2 Vasili I (1389-1425)
3 Vasili II (1425-1462)
4 Ivan III the Great
   (1462-1505)
5 Vasili III (1505-1533)
6 Ivan IV the Terrible
   (1533-1584)
7 Feodor I (1584-1598)
8 Boris Godunov
   (1598-1605)
9 Feodor II (1605)
10 False Dmitri I
   (1605-1606)
11 Vasili IV
   (1606-1610)
Interregnum (1610-1613)
12 Michael Romanov
   (1613-1645)
13 Alexis I (1645-1676)
14 Feodor III (1676-1682)
15 Ivan V and Peter the
   Great (1682-1696)
16 Peter the Great (alone)
   (1696-1724)
17 Peter the Great and
   Catherine I
   (1724- 1725)
18 Catherine I (1725-1727)
19 Peter II (1727-1730)
20 Anna (1730-1740)
21 Ivan VI (1740-1741)
22 Elizabeth (1741-1762)
23 Peter III (1762)
24 Catherine II the Great
   (1762-1796)
25 Paul I (1796-1801)
26 Alexander I
   (1801-1825)
27 Nicholas I (1825-1855)
28 Alexander II
   (1855-1881)
29 Alexander III
   (1881-1894)
30 Nicholas II (1894-1917)

RUSSIAN PRESIDENTS FROM 1918

1 Vladimir Ilyich Lenin
   (1918-1924)
2 Josef Stalin
   (1927-1953)
3 Nikita Khrushchev
   (1953-1964)

4 Leonid Ilyich Brezhnev
   (1964-1982)
5 Yuri Andropov
   (1983-1984)
6 Konstantin Chernenko
   (1984-1985)
7 Mikhail Gorbachev
   (1985-1991)
8 Boris Yeltsin
   (1991-1999)
9 Vladimir Putin (2000—

RULERS OF ENGLAND (TO 1603)

SAXONS

1 Egbert (827-839)
2 Ethelwulf (839-858)
3 Ethelbald (858-860)
4 Ethelbert (860-865)
5 Ethelred I (865-871)
6 Alfred the Great
   (871-899)
7 Edward the Elder
   (899-924)
8 Athelstan (924-939)
9 Edmund (939-946)
10 Edred (946-955)
11 Edwy (955-959)
12 Edgar (959-975)
13 Edward the Martyr
   (975-978)
14 Ethelred II the Unready
   (978-1016)
15 Edmund Ironside
   (1016)

DANES

1 Canute (1016-1035)
2 Harold I Harefoot
   (1035-1040)
3 Hardicanute (1040-1042)

SAXONS

1 Edward the Confessor
   (1042-1066)
2 Harold II (1066)

HOUSE OF NORMANDY

1 William I the Conqueror
   (1066-1087)
2 William II (1087-1100)
3 Henry I (1100-1135)
4 Stephen (1135-1154)

HOUSE OF PLANTAGENET

1 Henry II (1154-1189)
2 Richard I (1189-1199)
3 John (1199-1216)
4 Henry III (1216-1272)
5 Edward I (1272-1307)
6 Edward II (1307-1327)
7 Edward III (1327-1377)
8 Richard II (1377-1399)

HOUSE OF LANCASTER

1 Henry IV (1399-1413)
2 Henry V (1413-1422)
3 Henry VI (1422-1461) and (1470-1471)

HOUSE OF YORK

1 Edward IV (1461-1470) and (1471-1483)
2 Edward V (1483)

3 Richard III (1483-1485)

HOUSE OF TUDOR

1 Henry VII (1485-1509)
2 Henry VIII (1509-1547)
3 Edward VI (1547-1553)
4 Mary I (1553-1558)
5 Elizabeth I (1558-1603)

RULERS OF BRITAIN

HOUSE OF STUART

1 James I (1603-1625)
2 Charles I (1625-1649)
3 Commonwealth
   (1649-1660)

HOUSE OF STUART RESTORED

1 Charles II (1660-1685)
2 James II (1685-1688)
3 William III (1689-1702)
   jointly
4 Mary II (1689-1694)
5 Anne (1702-1714)

HOUSE OF HANOVER

1 George I (1714-1727)
2 George II (1727-1760)
3 George III (1760-1820)
4 George IV (1820-1830)
5 William IV (1830-1837)
6 Victoria (1837-1901)

HOUSE OF SAXE - COBURG

1 Edward VII (1901-1910)

HOUSE OF WINDSOR

1 George V (1910-1936)
2 Edward VIII (1936)
3 George VI (1936-1952)
4 Elizabeth II (1952—

RULERS OF SCOTLAND (to 1603)

1 Malcolm II (1005-1034)
2 Duncan I (1034-1040)
3 Macbeth (1040-1057)
4 Malcolm III Canmore
   (1058-1093)
5 Donald Bane
   (1093-1094)
6 Duncan II (1094)
7 Donald Bane (restored)
   (1094-1097)
8 Edgar (1097-1107)
9 Alexander I (1107-1124)
10 David I (1124-1153)
11 Malcolm IV
   (1153-1165)
12 William the Lion
   (1165-1214)
13 Alexander II
   (1214-1249)
14 Alexander III
   (1249-1286)
15 Margaret of Norway
   (1286-1290)
Interregnum (1290-1292)
16 John Balliol
   (1292-1296)
Interregnum (1296-1306)
17 Robert I (Bruce)
   (1306-1329)
18 David II (1329-1371)

HOUSE OF STUART

1 Robert II (1371-1390)
2 Robert III (1390-1406)
3 James I (1406-1437)
4 James II (1437-1460)
5 James III (1460-1488)
6 James IV (1488-1513)
7 James V (1513-1542)
8 Mary (1542-1567)
9 James VI
   (became James I of
   England in 1603)
   (1567-1625)

BRITISH PRIME MINISTERS

W = Whig; T = Tory;
L = Liberal; Lab = Labour;
C = Conservative.

1 Sir Robert Walpole (W)
   (1721-1742)
2 Earl of Wilmington (W)
   (1742-1743)
3 Henry Pelham (W)
   (1743-1754)
4 Duke of Newcastle (W)
   (1754-1756)
5 Duke of Devonshire (W)
   (1756-1757)
6 Duke of Newcastle (W)
   (1757-1762)
7 Earl of Bute (T)
   (1762-1763)
8 George Grenville (W)
   (1763-1765)
9 Marquis of Rockingham
   (W) (1765-1766)
10 William Pitt, 'The Elder'
   (W) (1766-1768)
11 Duke of Grafton (W)
   (1767-1770)
12 Lord North (T)
   (1770-1782)
13 Marquis of Rockingham
   (W)(1782)
14 Earl of Shelburne (W)
   (1782-1783)
15 Duke of Portland (T)
   (1783)
16 William Pitt,
   'The Younger' (T)
   (1783-1801)
17 Henry Addington (T)
   (1801-1804)
18 William Pitt
   'The Younger' (T)
   (1804-1806)
19 Lord Grenville (W)
   (1806-1807)
20 Duke of Portland (T)
   (1807-1809)
21 Spencer Perceval (T)
   (1809-1812)
22 Earl of Liverpool (T)
   (1812-1827)
23 George Canning (T)
   (1827)
24 Viscount Goderich (T)
   (1827-1828)
25 Duke of Wellington (T)
   (1828-1830)
26 Earl Grey (W)
   (1830-1834)
27 Viscount Melbourne
   (W) (1834)
28 Sir Robert Peel